PIT TO PALACE

SEVEN PROVEN PRINCIPLES FOR ULTIMATE SUCCESS

To: Cherie,
Thanks for All the love and support. You have the power to move mountains, use it!

DARRELL BARNES

PIT TO PALACE

Copyright © 2010 by Darrell Barnes

All rights reserved. No part of this publication may be reproduced, stored in a retrieval system, or transmitted in any form by means electronic, mechanical, photocopying, recording or otherwise, except for the inclusion of brief quotations in a review, without prior permission in writing from the publisher.

ISBN: 978-0-9824145-1-4

Published by

LifeBridge Books
P.O. BOX 49428
CHARLOTTE, NC 28277

Printed in the United States of America.

Dedication

First, I would like to thank the Creator of heaven and earth for entrusting me with this kingdom assignment.

I dedicate this book to my wife, Patricia, who saw in me that which I could not see in myself. This is just the beginning. I love you.

To my parents JoAnn and Travis and my girls Darian and Adreianna. You keep me grounded and never let me think too highly of myself.

To the best church family this side of heaven, The Community of Faith Church. You are truly a visible manifestation of the power of God in the presence of people.

Finally, to my spiritual father, Bishop James Dixon II. I thank you for speaking life into my dry bones. I can't wait to see where God takes us next.

To anyone who has had a hand in making me the man I am today, whether good or bad, past or present, I say thank you for the motivation.

Contents

Introduction	7
Part I	
An Unexpected Journey	13
Into the Pit	27
Part II	
Success Principle #1: Stop Where You Are and Change Directions	43
Success Principle #2: Believe in Yourself and Your Abilities	63
Success Principle #3: Develop a Game Plan	79
Success Principle #4: Discover Your Calling	93
Success Principle #5: Find a Successful Example to Follow	107
Success Principle #6: Have a Righteous Resolve	115
Success Principle #7: Possess the Palace	127
A Final Word	139

Introduction

Whdt you are about to read is not just an imaginary journey that takes you from a deep valley to a high mountain peak.

As you will learn, I know first hand what it means to live in a pit—to be thrown into a dark place for years, with no way of escape. But during the most disheartening days, I set a course for my future that includes the Seven Principles for Ultimate Success you are about to discover.

They transformed my life—and I believe they will dramatically revolutionize your future too.

Regardless of where you are on the ladder of life, when you begin to apply these principles, the steps to the top become shorter, safer, and much more satisfying.

Your Discovery

In this book you will learn:

- How to identify a wrong path so you can change directions.
- The keys to believing in yourself and your abilities.
- The secret of developing a personal game plan for your future.
- How to discover your calling and purpose for life.
- The importance of finding a mentor and an example to follow.
- The necessity of having a righteous resolve.
- How to claim the palace you deserve.

Personally, I am thrilled that you are reading this book. Why? Because I know in advance the impact it will have on you— today, tomorrow, and for the rest of your life.

An Ultimate Purpose

Before we get into the principles to practice, I want to share my story. There are parts of my journey I wish

I could erase from my memory, or from the pages of history. But looking back, I now see how these events served to uncover my ultimate purpose on this earth.

I am grateful for the opportunity to pour out my heart and transfer to you what God has so graciously given to me. It is my prayer that as a result of reading this book you will not just move from Pit to Palace, but plant the seeds of greatness into the lives of others.

– *Darrell Barnes*

PART I

Chapter One

An Unexpected Journey

Who has never tasted what is bitter does not know what is sweet.

– German Proverb

In reality, I shouldn't even be here!

My mother, JoAnn, had an encounter with ovarian cancer which left her with a prognosis from doctors that she would never have children. Yet, a little over five years after my parents were married, I came into this world. To my mom, it was a miracle.

The only conclusion I can come to is that the seed which had been planted in her womb had been purposed for a great work, which not even cancer could derail, defeat, or deny. I am the only child born to my mother and father.

Shortly after my birth, my father, Travis, made the choice to leave my mother and I. Later in life he described his decision to me as "Leaving for a better situation"—a statement I struggled to understand.

My father had been a civil servant for most of his adult life, being a bus driver for the city of Houston, Texas, for over thirty years. As such, he was looked up to in the community as a man of respect —partly because of the uniform he wore to work. For a black man of the late sixties and seventies, he made a respectable salary.

Just Me and Mom

My mother was a stay-at-home mom. We owned a house in the relatively new black middle-class section of Houston named South Park. The area had Houston's first shopping mall (or "plaza" as they called it then), Palm Center.

Mom was the third of eleven children. However,

my dad had been an only child after his sister Marcia died when she was very young. Both of my parents grew up in the rough, poor, but history-rich and pride-filled community called Acres Homes on the northwest side of town.

Once my father left our home, my mother had to fend for herself as well as her newborn baby. With me riding on her hip, Mom would catch a bus every day to look for a job. She eventually landed a position in the medical field as a surgical technician—a skill she had studied for. The pay was low, but she was thrilled for the opportunity. To this day I do not know who in their right mind would hire a woman who brought a baby to a job interview. I presume they felt sorry for us and just wanted to help.

> *The past is for inspiration, not imitation, for continuation, not repetition.*
> – I. Zangewill

A Display of Compassion

Eventually, because of our financial situation, we

had no other option than to move out of our home. Mom, who was twenty-five at the time, had no desire to move back in with her parents. My maternal grandparents still had their hands full with eight other children living in a six room house.

On the other side of the family, my paternal grandparents were empty nesters. One would expect, when a divorce occurs, family members take sides in accordance with their genealogical link to the divorced. However, my father's mother, Eva Barnes, generously made my mom an offer that would prove to be invaluable. To this day I am benefitting from her display of compassion.

To this day I am benefitting from her display of compassion.

Eva, along with my grandfather, Albert, owned the house next door to where they lived on Mansfield Street. They offered it to my mother at no cost for as long as she needed it. My father objected, but was overruled by my grandparents.

An Extended Family

As a result I spent most of my childhood in what was called Acres Homes on Mansfield Street. I clearly remember attending Antioch Baptist Church pre-school under the directorship of Ms. Cora Bell, then entering kindergarten at Highland Heights Elementary School.

My days were never dull or boring as I ran back and forth from my house to my grandparents' home next door. I also spent a considerable amount of time at my maternal grandmother's house, which was always overflowing with three or four of my cousins—after all, my maternal grandfather had twenty-five children, eleven with my grandmother.

> *Gladly accept the gifts of the present hour.*
> – Horace

A Foundation of Faith

Being a devout Christian, my mother raised me with the same beliefs that her mother Zelma had instilled in her. They were faithful members of the Church of God in Christ.

On dad's side, my grandmother, Eva, attended Antioch Baptist Church, serving under Dr. F. N. Williams, as did my grandfather, Albert Barnes—an associate minister, though he was a quadriplegic for most of those years.

We lived in the house on Mansfield Street for over ten years—rent free. During that time, my mother had accepted a position with Texas Instruments, a company which then was on the cutting edge of technology, much like Microsoft today. She worked her way up the ladder from an assembly line technician to a customer care associate with small raises along the way.

———⚜———
It must have been lonely for her as a single mom.

During these years, unknown to me, my mother had been saving a considerable part of her income and investing in the company stock options.

I knew it must have been lonely for her as a single mom, but in those years I had only known my mother to date one man briefly. She never allowed any male friend to stay overnight at our house. She was a woman of honor and integrity who always put her son first.

There was one guy I was familiar with, Alvin. He was really cool, drove a fast Corvette, and dressed really sharp. I have no idea what happened to him or why they stopped seeing each other.

> *She was a woman of honor and integrity who always put her son first.*

My New Dad

As I think back, considerable time passed from Alvin to the day my mother sat me down and broke the news that she was getting married—and we would be moving.

I was only eight years old and had no idea what being married really meant other than I would have a man in the house who would serve the role of dad to those on the outside looking in. It never registered with me that he would become *my dad.*

I felt good over the realization that my family would now have the appearance of what I had seen on television. To be honest, I had been holding the title of "man of the house" for quite a while and did harbor a little resentment at relinquishing my title to someone I hardly knew. After all, who did he think he was?

Deep down, I felt this was going to be a problem.

Deep down, I felt this was going to be a problem. Ironically, it was no trouble at all. Robert "Bobby" McGarthy was the first man I ever respected—period.

An Answer to Prayer

It was not until I became a man that I realized what a blessing he had been to me and my mother. Mom told me she prayed for such a husband and God answered her prayer.

They were married for twenty-four years until his

untimely death on Thanksgiving day, 2004. By that time I was married and had a three-month-old daughter.

Unfortunately, he would never get to see my purpose fulfilled on this earth.

> *Unfortunately, he would never get to see my purpose fulfilled on this earth.*

IMMERSED IN SPORTS

In school, I made average grades, played football, basketball, and ran track. In the summer I was on the baseball team. My mom and Bobby cheered me on and never missed a game.

Eventually basketball became my focus. I began to excel in the sport and started looking at scholarship opportunities because I knew my parents were not in a position to pay for a college education. My coach liked and encouraged me. I was the only 10th grader to make the varsity in the history of the school. Though we didn't have a great team, I was making a name for myself. At the end of my sophomore season I was given the award: "Newcomer of the Year."

All summer I worked to improve on last year's performance. I attended camps and summer leagues to make myself accessible to college coaches. However, I came back to school in the fall to find out that our coach was not returning. His replacement wanted to go in another direction that did not include me. I was crushed!

Playing for a Winner

———✤———
This is the first time I recall God pushing me in a certain direction.

As I look back, this is the first time I recall God pushing me in a certain direction. During these days my biological father was living in my grandparents' house on Mansfield Street. My grandfather, Albert, had passed on several years earlier and my grandmother retired to her home town in east Texas. My father, Travis, suggested I transfer to his (and my mother's) alma mater, Booker

T. Washington high school—a predominately, and historically black school in the Studewood section of Houston.

It did not take much to convince me. I had been following their basketball team the year before and they had one of the better squads in the city.

During my senior year I made good grades at Washington and our team went all the way to the state quarter-finals. Even though we didn't win it all, it felt exhilarating playing for a winner.

Regarding scholarships, I only received offers from small colleges, so I made the decision to enroll at division I-A, Texas Tech, as a walk-on.

Even then, God was positioning me for what was ahead.

As a result of my transfer from my old school to Washington, my class ranking went from two hundred and something to graduating in the top ten percent of my class. Even then God was positioning me for what was ahead.

A Financial Surprise

I was admitted to Texas Tech, in Lubbock,

unconditionally—meaning no probationary period and no mandatory minimum grades for me to keep up.

The Lord had removed every obstacle. It is amazing, since Texas Tech was the only school to which I had made application. Theoretically, it was either there or nowhere for me. Actually, I had no burning desire to attend college, but because of my mother's dream for me, I pursued it half-heartedly. Imagine my surprise reading an acceptance letter that stated not only was I admitted but without conditions.

> *There was still a nagging question as to how I was going to pay for college.*

There was still a nagging question as to how I was going to pay for college. Our household income between my mother and Bobby exceeded the maximum limit to qualify for a grant.

My only option, I thought, was for my parents to take out a loan.

But there was something I did not know. As a result of my grandmother Eva's benevolence regarding housing some eighteen years earlier, my mother explained that she was able to save and put aside funds for my education. God had given her vision, a plan of action, as well as someone such as Eva Barnes, who used her power, influence, and ability to help make my mother's dream for her son come true. (See Exodus 36:3-5).

However, I had no idea of the pitfalls on the road ahead which would detour me.

Chapter Two

Into the Pit

*When it is dark enough,
you can see the stars.*

– Ralph Waldo Emerson

I have always had an entrepreneurial spirit latent within me—but, as you will learn, it contributed to a personal downfall.

My family tree is filled with branches of ancestors who were dentists, pharmacists, grocers, even a funeral home director. My cousin Timothy Barnes is the oldest licensed mortician in the state of Texas at over ninety years of age. His father was owner and founder of Carl Barnes Funeral Home, an institution in the Houston community for over forty years.

Because of my lack of spiritual awareness at the

time, what God meant for good—my skills as a entrepreneur—the devil manipulated for his own purpose.

It all seemed to happen at once. During my freshman year at Texas Tech, I began to experiment with alcohol and marijuana.

I fell in with the wrong crowd and before long was indoctrinated into low-level street mentality. These so-called friends introduced me to forms of making money illegally. I became involved with forgery, fraud, as well as playing con games.

> *I fell in with the wrong crowd and before long was indoctrinated into low-level street mentality.*

Yes, my mother paid for my tuition, but my expenses and spending money were obtained by illegal means. Those who knew me in those days will tell you that I always kept a hefty "bank roll" in my pocket.

A Rough Image

Most students who observed me on campus

probably perceived me as a thug or gangster. I was constantly involved in fights with other drug dealers, gang members from the community, as well as some students on campus. At one point I found it necessary to carry a gun.

Even though a lot of the guys at Tech didn't particularly like me, somehow the girls saw an attraction—although I'm sure many of them must have questioned my behavior.

In spite of my rebellious actions and poor attitude, I still managed to keep my grades up to a decent level.

In spite of my rebellious actions and poor attitude, I still managed to keep my grades up to a decent level.

MY REFUGE

Although I was caught up in activities I knew were wrong, deep inside there was a tugging at my heart—something pulling me back toward the foundation that had been my refuge as a child. I found myself unable to ignore these feelings any longer, so I began visiting several churches in the Lubbock area.

The ministry at one small Church of God in Christ that I attended really made an impression on me. So much so that one Sunday Morning I was moved to walk down the aisle toward the altar where I rededicated my life to Christ and made a vow to make a change for the better.

It was the Agape Love Church, where Reverend William Watson, was the presiding bishop. I even started attending Bible study on Friday nights at 11:00 P.M. The church wanted to provide an alternative to parties, night clubs, and drinking associated with college life.

The church wanted to provide an alternative to parties, night clubs, and drinking associated with college life.

Bill Watson, Bishop Watson's son, whom I had a class with, was the moderator. Only ten or twelve students ever showed up, but I became a regular. It was my place of refuge.

A Hand of Protection

As I reflect back on that troubled period in my life, I thank God for my mother and her grounded teachings. Though I was active in things I am now deeply ashamed of, I realize I was never far from the arms of God. His hand of protection and grace always reached out to me.

> *Though I was active in things I am now deeply ashamed of, I realize I was never far from the arms of God.*

Even when I was involved with drugs and other illegal activities, I managed to stay clear of law enforcement. However, a fraternity brother and myself were placed on disciplinary probation for assaulting another student in retaliation for an attack on one of our own fraternity brothers.

Despite it all, it was with a great sense of accomplishment I proudly graduated from Texas Tech with a Bachelor of Arts degree.

"Bad Actors"

My move back to Houston in the summer of 1995 was not all peaches and cream. Trying to be accepted by my peers, I soon drifted back into the sordid lifestyle of the street and smoking marijuana—my drug of choice.

I was hanging out with a group of guys I knew from high school who some would call "bad actors." We would waste countless hours in a housing complex where several of them shared an apartment. They were involved in everything from burglary and auto theft, to dealing narcotics, but in the early days of being back in Houston, I wasn't an active participant in any of their illegal activities.

One reason I tried to avoid trouble was that I had moved back home with my mother and step-father, and had more respect for them than I did for myself. I would never intentionally bring shame upon their house.

Sadly, even with my university degree in hand, I had zero luck finding employment. After a couple of months of searching for a job with no success, I resorted back to dealing drugs. I sold narcotics to my friends, and even some family members who promised not to tell my mother the truth of what I was doing.

A Surprising Sunday

During those difficult days, one event became a real turning point. At the invitation of my God-sister, Deavra, I visited a church she had recently joined.

Looking back brings a smile to my face when I recall the first time I turned onto the street where Deavra's church was located. I saw black men of all ages and shapes lined up and down the street greeting passers by and inviting them to join them in worship that Sunday morning. I was simply amazed at the sight of over fifty or more black men in forest green blazers with the

During those difficult days, one event became a real turning point.

church logo embroidered on the pocket. They were lined up for the three or four blocks it took me to make it into the parking lot.

These brothers were directing traffic, helping with parking, and even opening doors for the women when they pulled up. I simply could not believe what I was seeing.

Though I had been home from college a few months, I had visited my home church only once or twice and didn't seem to connect. Spiritually, I was seeking more, but had no idea what it was.

I remember once telling my mother, "I think the devil is trying to kill me."

Thankfully, she kept me in her prayers.

> *I remember once telling my mother, "I think the devil is trying to kill me."*

WHO WAS THIS MAN?

On that memorable Sunday morning, as I walked into a church called "Community of Faith," I felt there was a certain something about the people in attendance which seemed so different than those at my home church, or even my grandparents' churches. They were not even like my loving family at the Agape Love Church in Lubbock, but I could not put my finger on what that distinction was. I just hoped that the pastor was not one of the Cadillac-driving, gold-chain-wearing, spitting-in-your-face kind of preachers I'd seen so often on television!

When I entered the sanctuary and took a seat, I couldn't help but notice how cordial everyone was. I also observed that choir did not wear the traditional robes, just their own Sunday clothes. This was new to me.

Out of the corner of my eye I saw a door open and a man followed by another entered the auditorium and walked up to the platform. My eyes followed them as the second man stopped and sat in

> *I just hoped that the pastor was not one of the Cadillac-driving, gold-chain-wearing, spitting-in-your-face kind of preachers I'd seen so often on television!*

the chair reserved for the pastor. I was again surprised because this individual didn't seem to be much older than I was.

He was dressed rather subdued—a simple dark suit with a non-flashy tie. There was no display of gaudy jewelry. The gentleman wasn't very tall, however his demeanor told me he was totally in command.

Dealing with the mix of people I had been around and having "street smarts," I was pretty adept at judging and assessing a person's motives rather quickly.

> *I was pretty adept at judging and assessing a person's motives rather quickly.*

A Spiritual Father

That morning, I was still skeptical, but remained optimistic. As he concluded his message, I found myself anxious to hear more of what God had imparted into this servant to give to me. He was definitely a spiritual motivator.

I returned to the church again and again and it was

not long until God began seriously dealing with me. I was unable to refuse His call to repent and connect with the vision that was being preached at the Community of Faith.

The pastor, who became my spiritual father, was Bishop James W.E. Dixon II. I was—and am to this day—one hundred percent in support of my bishop and his vision.

Immediately, after making the decision to call this my church home, I stopped selling drugs, drinking, and hanging out with my friends in the apartment they rented.

I stopped selling drugs, drinking, and hanging out with my friends in the apartment they rented.

My new routine was simple, yet exciting. I went to Bible study on Tuesday, new members orientation class on Friday, and service on Sunday.

"How Do You Plead?"

Almost a year to the day I accepted Christ back into my life, I was faced with a devastating personal crisis.

It was a dilemma no one should have to go through.

One of the young men from the group I used to hang out with and myself were charged with having sexual relations with two young women we had met when I was frequenting the guys apartment.

To the prosecutors, it was a simple open and shut case. They were minors and we were going to prison.

Guilt or innocence was not the question. My attorney told me I had only two choices. He said, "If we fight the charges and you lose, you will spend 20 years in jail. But if you plead guilty, you will avoid a trial and get probation. What do you want to do?"

As I quickly learned that day, there are serious consequences for associating with the wrong crowd.

There was no other option.

In open court, the judge stated the girls were "troubled runaways who were deceptive in their actions"—and as a result he would accept my plea.

Imagine my horror when I heard him further say that my actions warranted me being remanded into custody to serve a sentence of six years.

As I quickly learned that day, there are serious consequences for associating with the wrong crowd. Outwardly, it appeared that the enemy of my soul had won a victory—or so he thought! But I had absorbed enough truth in my one year of sitting under a strong ministry that my faith could not be compromised.

Even though I was literally headed for six years in a "pit" for a crime I did not commit, in my inner man I just knew God had much more in store.

Part II

Seven Proven Principles for Ultimate Success

Proven Principle for Ultimate Success

#1

Stop Where You Are and Change Directions

The journey of a million miles begins with one step.

– Lao Tzu

One of the most difficult things for us to do is move away from what is familiar. It is encoded in our DNA for us to stick to "known" territory—family, friends, and even the way we handle finances. But if you are serious about a successful future, whatever your situation, whatever your need, you must stop and make a conscious decision if you desire to change your circumstances.

> *You must stop and make a conscious decision if you desire to change your circumstances.*

First, you must have such a strong hunger to be released from your pit—whatever it may be—that you will do virtually anything to make change happen.

"The Light Bulb Went Off"

When I speak of a pit I am not referring to the physical manifestation of a naturally formed or excavated hole in the ground, but of the psychological place you have confined yourself. Likewise, when I mention financial well being, I not only mean having wealth or an abundance of possessions, but also, joy, love, contentment and happiness. These attributes are also manifestations of a prosperous lifestyle.

When this finally clicked for me, when, as they say,

"the light bulb went off" I was ready to make the transition.

It was sudden. I never second-guessed myself, and more importantly, I never looked back.

I never second-guessed myself, and more importantly, I never looked back.

I am a product of the Hip Hop generation and I am proud of this and make no apologies for it. While some have taken it to extremes, Hip Hop is pure. Rap music is a raw, uncut reflection of how young people use spoken words to express themselves.

Because of Hip Hop's authenticity, fakes, imposters, and infiltrators are easily identified. And once you are labeled as not being real, your credibility is gone.

So when speaking to young people, we must be obviously transparent with them or risk being tuned out. The phrase "real talk" means truth. Truth is truth—even when it hurts.

WE ALL NEED HELP

Whatever circumstance you find yourself in that calls for you to break free, you must first take immediate action to remove yourself from the situation. Do not wait until you muster the strength to "get yourself together."

> *Do not wait until you muster the strength to "get yourself together."*

Let's face it: if you could pull yourself together you would have already done so! Your "pit" is bigger than you are. No person has ever been down deep in a pit and had the ability to see out of it or climb out of it all by themselves. If he had then it was not a pit. At one time or another, we all need help.

No successful person reached their place of prominence alone: not Donald Trump, nor Bishop T.D. Jakes, not even Oprah.

No man is an island. If you want to birth a business or live a life free of drugs, you have to envision yourself in a new situation. You have to move—

mentally, physically, and spiritually.

Stop hanging out with the old crowd. Enter into a circle of people who live clean, ethical lives and know where they are headed. For example, if you plan to launch an enterprise, spend every possible moment with men or women who own a business, or who are at least like yourself, looking to go into business.

> *Stop hanging out with the old crowd.*

An Unswerving Decision

Before I was released from prison in 2002, I would sit around and listen to guys talk about their plans when they made it back to the outside world. Of the hundreds of men I spoke with, few, if any, mentioned anything of making real, substantive changes.

On the other hand, I had decided the only thing I was going to do was reunite with my newfound friends at Community of Faith and Bishop Dixon. I thought about this every waking moment. In my mind, I had already made the change—an unswerving decision of how I was going to conduct my life.

Reconnecting with my old "street" friends was out of the question. Day after day, in that prison cell, I prayed and asked God what He had in store for my future. I read my Bible constantly.

CHANGING FROM THE INSIDE OUT

> *I made some personal commitments of how I would present myself to the outside world.*

In addition to spiritual matters, I made some personal commitments of how I would present myself to the outside world. For example, I decided that once I was released I would dress in a professional manner everyday—even if I had nowhere to go. Professionally to me meant a shirt, tie, slacks, and what most people call "church shoes"—polished shoes that as a kid I was only allowed to wear to church.

Even in my cell, I was already mentally changing directions.

My favorite book says that, *"Death and life are in the power of the tongue"* (Proverbs 18:21). For that reason I began to speak myself out of my situation.

> *Even in my cell, I was already mentally changing directions.*

Each morning, as I would leave my cell block and head to my assigned task, I would speak positive affirmations, or what I now call "faith confessions" to myself:

- "I am a winner, not a looser."
- "Failure is not an option."
- "I am successful at whatever I do."
- "I am a positive influence to those around me."
- "Everything is getting better every day."

Even more, I began to quote passages from scripture that declare who I am as a child of God:

- "I am the head and not the tail...above and not beneath" (Deuteronomy 28:13).
- "Greater is He that is in me that he that is in the world" (1 John 4:4).
- "I can do all things through Christ who strengthens me" (Philippians 4:13).
- "My God shall supply all my need according to his riches in glory" (Philippians 4:19).
- "I walk by faith and not by sight" (2 Corinthians 5:7).
- "God is able to do exceedingly, abundantly, above all that I ask or think, according to the power that works in me" (Ephesians 3:20).
- "No weapon formed against me shall prosper" (Isaiah 54:17).
- "The joy of the Lord is my strength" (Nehemiah 8:10).

A Total Transformation

Slowly, and over time, people started to act

positively toward me. Not solely on the words that I spoke, but because I was becoming who I said I was—and what God declared me to be.

My attitude did a complete turn-around, and therefore my disposition was transformed.

Regardless of where you are in life, if you change your vocabulary you will eventually hear the words you are saying—and *become* those words, for good or bad.

> *Regardless of where you are in life, if you change your vocabulary you will eventually hear the words your are saying.*

A Letter to the Warden

While I was incarcerated there was a rule that no inmate was allowed tennis shoes purchased from the outside. The Texas Department of Criminal Justice sold their own brand of shoe. Because of security threats and uniformity, all inmates (if they desired tennis shoes) were required to make their purchase from the unit commissary.

I had been on the unit basketball team and we had won several tournaments. In the process, from simple wear and tear, I ruined every pair of shoes I purchased. They were cheaply made.

One day I was looking through the catalog of an athletic equipment company and decided to ask the warden if I could purchase my next pair of tennis shoes from this company. I had never spoken with the unit warden or even thought he knew who I was.

Because I was about to speak truth to power, I started quoting scriptures to myself: "No weapon formed against me shall prosper," and "Whatever you ask in Jesus' name, it shall be yours."

I sent the warden a letter detailing my request. Less than a week later the property officer called me into her office. I will never forget her name—Ms. Heck. She had my letter in her hands and the first thing she told me was,"I don't know how you were able to have the warden approve having shoes sent in from the outside. Every other request of this nature has been denied—and has been for years."

I just smiled and replied, "All things are possible for those who believe."

No More Excuses

There is no way I can know what you are struggling through at this very moment, but I can tell you with assurance that you have the power to change course and to speak things into your life.

It's sad to think that so few are aware that they possess the ability to re-route the course of their journey—not just a little, but drastically.

I've heard so many men and women complain, "I can't do that because my momma was a drug addict." Or because, "My daddy ran off and left me."

Believe me when I say it's time to stop making excuses as to why you cannot be successful.

It's time to stop making excuses as to why you cannot be successful.

When I was at Texas Tech and pledging the greatest fraternity in the world, we would have what we called "sessions." During *sessions*, under extreme pressure, we had to recite poetry verbatim and history as it relates to the fraternity. If you had an excuse as to why you were not able to perfect these lessons, one of the brothers would state emphatically, "Excuses are made by incompetent individuals to build a monument of nothingness."

"Excuses are made by incompetent individuals to build a monument of nothingness."

That was two decades ago. To this day, if I hear an individual offer an excuse for whatever reason, I silently mouth those words. Sometimes I will even repeat them out loud to the person making the excuse.

A Price to Pay

No matter what stop sign you are stalled at in life, there is always room for redirection or advancement. Most important is to know that you will never arrive at your desired destination until you first decide "there" is where you want to be.

At whatever cost—friends, family, or discomfort—there is always a price to pay to get out of your pit. Yes, you will get a little dirt on your hands climbing out, and you will strain your muscles to reach daylight. You may even get your clothes ripped or torn.

I can tell you from personal experience the escape will be uncomfortable. If not, you are not moving, growing, or developing. Rarely will you reach your purposed place through ease or comfort.

To Grandmother's House

After six long years I was released from prison with only a brown paper bag containing a toothbrush, toothpaste, and some letters I kept. I had no money, no job, no presentable clothes, and only a few family members to depend on. All I had was my faith and a plan.

My first stop upon release was my grandmother's

house. (While incarcerated I had lost my paternal grandmother and maternal grandfather). I had not seen her once during the years I had been gone. This strong woman who had prayed for and nurtured me from infancy to adulthood was now confined to a wheelchair. As I knelt at her feet to hug her, tears began to flow from both of us.

My next stop was my mother's home where I would live. It served as the base for my comeback. Being a grown man now living with family was not an easy transition. I felt like such a burden to her and my step-father.

Quite a Drastic Change

Upon my release, which was on a Friday, my uncle Delton took me to the store and bought me a couple of pairs of shoes. The next evening my God-sister Deavra asked me to accompany her to a fundraiser, which was to be held at a very elegant hotel. The event was to benefit then mayoral candidate and state representative Sylvester Turner.

I had been given money from my mother and a

few other people to purchase some things I needed. I ended up buying a suit, dress shirt, and tie.

Again, I was broke, but I had something to wear to a job interview when one came along. Most people upon release from prison will blow the little money they have on drugs, liquor, and women in no particular order. But those six years were not wasted on me. I had a plan and a goal.

> *Those six years were not wasted on me. I had a plan and a goal.*

OUT OF MY COMFORT ZONE

Prior to my release I had been praying that the Lord was going to place me in the company of people who would use their power and influence to help me.

Here I was, one day removed from eating and sleeping with the most feared offenders in the state, to rubbing elbows with movers and shakers of Texas and Washington politics. I met Congresswoman Sheila Jackson Lee that night for the first time. I also was introduced to some of the city's most influential politicians.

I must say that I worked the room pretty well for a person who, at that time, had never cast a ballot in an election. Later that would also change.

Some of the people I met that night I later called on. They have been a benefit to me as I have volunteered on their campaigns and service projects. This all happened because I took a bold step forward and accepted the invitation to go somewhere I would have previously been uncomfortable. I was willing to step out of my comfort zone to grow and move in the direction God had intended for me.

CIRCUMSTANCES DON'T MATTER

On Sunday I was back at Community of Faith—drinking in the Word of God I had deeply missed for so long. Oh, how happy I was to reunite with my church family.

At home, my mom and step-dad did what they

could for me but again, if you want to move from your pit to the palace, you can't get comfortable.

You may ask, "How could you speak positive affirmations while still living under the roof of another individual?"

Well, if I could speak that way behind bars, what made this temporary stopping place any different?

It is not your circumstances that define your place in life, but how you react to them.

> *It's not your circumstances that define your place in life, but how you react to them.*

My plan was to initially lay low and not let any of my old street friends know I was home.

As it turned out, that task was easier than expected. Most of my old crew were incarcerated with lengthy prison terms themselves. While some of the guys I once hung out with had straightened out their lives, others were dead.

In the neighborhood there was a new young group out on the streets. They had no idea who I was and I preferred it that way.

Life at "The Office"

Next, I needed a job. I checked the classifieds and I learned to use the Internet. I had taken an introductory computer class before my release. As a result I was able to navigate the World Wide Web as if I had been doing it for years. Still, despite my newly acquired skill, I had no luck finding work.

I continued to pray and speak confessions of faith daily believing that the opportunity I wanted would come along. Every day I would go to the public library and use their computers to email my resume and to surf the web. There were days I would be at the library for eight to ten hours, so I began calling it my office!

Anytime someone would ask me were I was going I would reply, "the office." One of the reasons I said this was because I believed God for a job with a computer and my own office.

I went to job fairs I would read about in the

newspaper and continued my search.

As you will learn later in this book, success is more than a job. God will open the right doors to place you exactly where He wants you to be.

Today, because of what I have encountered, I am able to tell people who are headed down the wrong path, "Stop where you are, and change directions."

You may not enjoy every mile of the journey, but if you choose your destination wisely, your purpose will erase every pain.

PROVEN PRINCIPLE FOR ULTIMATE SUCCESS

#2

BELIEVE IN YOURSELF AND YOUR ABILITIES

Nothing splendid has ever been achieved except by those who dared believe that something inside them was superior to circumstances.

– BRUCE BARTON

Never in a million years would I have gone to that fundraiser if I felt I was going to embarrass myself or Deavra.

You must be fearless in order to move to that promised place God has prepared for you on this earth. You must believe that what you are doing is beneficial to the ultimate vision God has given you—which in turn is the goal you have set to achieve.

Perhaps the greatest mistake I see young people make is wasting time on something that does not matter. Let me explain. What would have happened if, instead of allowing my uncle to take me shopping for shoes, I thought it was more fun to go to a ball game with a buddy? What if I had been too busy trying to track down an old girlfriend? My preoccupation in trivial things would have been valuable time wasted.

In order to find your place of prosperity you absolutely must be focused and disciplined.

In order to find your place of prosperity you absolutely must be focused and disciplined. Once you train yourself to master these factors, most other things will fall into line.

I have not chewed gum in over ten years—yet as a young person I popped it in my mouth all the time. How did this habit change? While in prison, where gum is prohibited, I realized that even though I enjoyed gum, it was not a life-sustaining necessity. In fact, my teeth and gums are probably much better off without it!

What do You Love?

The journey to self-esteem and prosperity requires getting to know the real you and what your assets are. Have a serious talk with yourself and ask the question: "What do I excel at?"

Make a list of five things people say you have a talent for. Then circle three of them that you really enjoy—and cross off the rest. You now have three skills you are proficient at and love doing.

Follow Your Interest

One of my jobs after coming out of prison was being a recruiter of high school students at a Vocational Training School. My assignment was that I go into the schools and give presentations to the students to show them their opportunity. Many of the young people teachers referred to me were borderline low-academic performers who most school administrators had declared unlikely to be four-year college material.

After conversations with the students and even some of their parents, it was evident these were not dumb kids. They simply were not turned on by what the teachers had to offer.

Most of my presentations were to vocational classes, where the students learn hands-on skills. I would ask for the phone numbers of the students who showed the most interest in our programs in order to set up future interviews with their parents.

Of the students I qualified based on what I believed their interest level in our programs were, almost 85% graduated. That was and still is a very high number.

As a result of my experience working with these kids I surmised that based on their commitment level, they were more likely to show up for class, ask questions, and exert greater effort. Simply because they were motivated by what they were learning, they made better grades. In reality, they were no smarter than any of the other students.

Find "It"

You have to ignite a spark and passion internally for what you do for a living. If you do not, you must treat the job as temporary income and find a way to pursue what you really love. Once you define what that *it* is, I guarantee you will be successful.

Once you define what it is, I guarantee you will be successful.

Wealth will follow when you delight in what you do. Why? Because without being asked or even thinking about it, you will work hard at the task when a disinterested person will not. As a result you will be rewarded financially. The key that unlocks the door called Success is believing in yourself.

I love the poem "IF" by Rudyard Kipling. My favorite stanza is the first, which reads, *"IF you can keep your head when all about you are losing theirs and blaming it on you."* After a dozen more "IF's, his poem concludes, "*IF you can fill the unforgiving minute, with sixty seconds' worth of distance run, Yours is the Earth and everything that's in it. And—which is more—you'll be a Man, my son!*"

These inspiring words have helped me through many difficult hours.

LET FAITH ARISE

There is no alternative; you must believe in your own abilities. My Bishop, James Dixon II, has taught me, *"Faith is my uncompromised belief in God's ability to perform on my behalf despite the opposition."*

Let me encourage you to have this truth so deeply ingrained in your psyche that when opposition and obstacles present themselves, you immediately let faith kick into action. This does not happen overnight. At least it wasn't that way for me. I had to continually work at it. And, to be honest, I still have to focus to keep doubt from slipping into my thought process.

At times of uncertainty, I still catch myself speaking

negatively, but immediately I am convicted. Just as quickly, I speak a confession of faith and get back to my rightful place.

LET GOD HANDLE THE DETAILS

A friend once shared with me, "There are times when you have to believe in someone else's faith in you, until your own faith kicks in."

Always remember: Whatever your desire in life, God can afford your dreams.

> *Whatever your desire in life, God can afford your dreams.*

If your lifelong ambition is to be an entrepreneur, singer, attorney, engineer, police officer, school bus driver, it is possible. The number one prerequisite for success is that you must first believe in yourself and your ability to perform. The Lord will handle the details.

I can guarantee that if you fail to take action or are too afraid to step out in faith, your dream will never materialize. My mentor in the business world is renowned motivational speaker Les Brown. He always reminds me to *"Live full and die empty."*

What he means by this statement is: do not let your dreams become buried in the grave with the shell of your physical body after death.

> *Live full and die empty.*
> – Les Brown

Many young people, as well as those who are older in years, depart from the earth each day without ever fulfilling their potential.

A Spirit of Expectancy

I started a real estate investment company as well as a custom home building firm with no bank account. I began with just a seed of an idea. Next, I had business cards printed with the company's names. In addition, I began to talk to people about what I hoped to do—only I spoke as if it already existed.

I had a spirit of expectancy.

I would wake in the morning and say to myself, "I will buy several pieces of property today." Whether I was able to accomplish this or not before the sun went down was never an indication of success for me. If I was unsuccessful that particular day, I would simply remind myself, *"'No' is only 'no' for today."*

"'No' is only 'no' for today."

I have since purchased properties with a ten dollar earnest money contract. I speak favor upon my business. I have no need to place large sums of money in escrow to purchase or execute a contract of sale.

It simply goes back to two things I adamantly believe in: (1) God's ability to perform on my behalf and (2) my belief in my own abilities.

Never Talk About Problems

If an obstacle rears its ugly head, never use the word *problem* to describe or categorize it. Go to God and make a faith demand. I speak to the Almighty like this: "You said you would diminish my enemies' ability to hurt me and You would remove every stumbling block. I have done my part. I have sown seed in good ground. I have given first fruit offerings. Now I need You to remove this obstacle."

You have to be convinced in your heart that there are no problems—only minor obstacles that are easily overcome.

Forget about the circumstances. Everything begins with your faith and confidence to take charge. It all starts with this mindset.

> *There are no problems, only minor obstacles that are easily overcome.*
> – Darrell Barnes

SPECIFIC—ABOUT A WIFE

Before my release from prison, I spoke to the Lord concerning a wife and family. After so many years out of social circulation, the women I had dated had found others and moved on with their relationships. One in particular I had feelings for, but I refused to hurt or string her along during my lengthy prison sentence. Others I did correspond with on and off during those troubled years.

I was anxious for a new start and asked God for

four things in a wife that I knew I needed in order to remain committed to the relationship. In my early days, I had never been taught to speak to God directly. Those around me seemed to always pray "general" prayers.

It was not until I was placed under the ministry of Bishop Dixon that I learned I could be specific concerning my wants and needs.

Over the years, the Holy Spirit was leading me and I didn't realize it. I thought I was brilliant enough to come up with all of these clever ideas myself. As vain as it may sound, the four things I asked God for in my future wife were these:

1. A woman who was pleasing to my eyes.
2. A woman who would accept my past.
3. A woman who simply loved me for me.
4. A woman who loved the Lord.

Patricia had each of the qualities I petitioned God for.

In the past, there were young ladies who seemed to have an agenda when dating me. That was okay because I realized the friendship was only temporary.

But that formula never makes for a lasting relationship.

A Reconnection

I believe as a direct result of my specific prayer, Patricia Jackson showed up in my life for the second time.

Statistically speaking, most people find their mate during their college years. Patricia and I met almost fifteen years earlier when I enrolled as a new student at Washington High School. At the time I thought she was nice but never entertained the idea of dating her, because I felt she had no interest in me—to say the least.

It was years later before we met again at church and reconnected. It was the same church where I dedicated my life to the Lord seven years earlier.

In the Bible, seven is the number of completion. I have never felt more complete than the day she accepted my hand in marriage.

How Big Do You Dream?

If I did not believe in myself and my ability to provide for a wife based on my past circumstance I would have never asked Patricia to marry me.

It is important to get this vital principle down deep in your spirit: "Believe in Yourself and Your Abilities."

You need more than a degree to get the promotion you seek on your job. You need favor from God, and the belief that you can accomplish the task effectively.

In addition, you don't need a large sum of money to step out on faith to start that business which is burning in your heart. Be convinced of your potential to run that successful company. Let me encourage you to read *Purpose to Blessing* by Deavra Daughtry. It's available at www.Amazon.com.

She is an up-close example for me of what you can do if you believe in your abilities to achieve exceptional success.

God will never bless you beyond your ability to picture great things.

Fulfilling this principle begins with you. How big do you dream? God will never bless you beyond your ability to picture great things.

75

Have Faith for Favor

I once heard it stated, "There are blessings in heaven that have yet to be prayed for."

Think about that for a moment? Can you imagine arriving in heaven and being shown all of your blessings and favors that were being stored because they were beyond your capability to envision?

> *"There are blessings in heaven that have yet to be prayed for."*

Many of us, especially black people, do not believe we deserve nice homes, jobs, cars, bank accounts, etc.

When a man of God stands and reveals to us in scripture concerning having the desires of our heart, he is labeled a prosperity preacher. However, when an entertainer or professional athlete buys a Rolls Royce they are applauded for being successful. Even Christians rally around such individuals and celebrate them.

What troubles me is these same people gossip, backbite, and belittle the minister when God elevates him to a place where he can own a Bentley automobile. What we should be saying *is, "I need to get closer to him in ministry. I want the same favor he has with God."*

The anointing flows from the top down. Get in a position to be blessed in the overflow.

Today, start believing in yourself. Have faith in your abilities—your lifeline to the future. God can afford your dreams.

PROVEN PRINCIPLE FOR ULTIMATE SUCCESS

#3

DEVELOP A GAME PLAN

Setting a goal is not the main thing. It is deciding how you will go about achieving it and staying with that plan.

– TOM LANDRY

I recently met a young woman who told me how she was in an abusive marriage for many years. She was abused verbally as well as physically until one night she found herself pressed against the wall of her home by her husband—with the barrel of a handgun shoved in her mouth.

Flooded with memories of that horrific evening, she

said, "I instinctively began to pray that God would shield me and not let me die from a bullet."

As her husband pulled the trigger, God miraculously answered her prayer.

The bullet lodged in her jaw and broke a number of her teeth. But despite her injuries, she survived. She has undergone several surgeries to reconstruct her face, and still has challenges ahead with her speech.

Her husband will spend the better part of the remainder of his life in prison.

I asked the woman, who is the mother of several small children, how was she able to pick up the pieces after such a brutal attack. She explained that while still lying in the hospital, her only thoughts were for her children and how they were solely dependant on her. She had to devise a plan to get her life back on track—and made the decision that she did not want to be viewed the rest of her life as the victim.

While in a hospital bed, she took a pen to paper and began to write down the things that she had to do, in order of priority. This was important since even the smallest detail can be taken for granted or overlooked if we do not write them down.

Your Road Map

Because of my life experiences, I began to be invited to speak to groups of troubled teens and to inmates in prisons across the country. I spoke of the "Essential Elements of Transition," which has now evolved into what you are reading, the "Seven Proven Principles of Ultimate Success."

No matter your plight, place, or disposition, these principles are no respecter of person. Whoever chooses to apply them will achieve their desired result.

Even though I believed I stumbled upon these principles by chance, I now know beyond a shadow of doubt the Holy Spirit guided me.

I have talked to many successful people the last couple of years and each of them have applied these very precepts, knowingly or unknowingly,

No matter your plight, place, or disposition, these principles are no respecter of person.

to achieve whatever level of success they have obtained.

When I mention success, transitioning from an abusive relationship with one person to a rewarding relationship with another doesn't happen by osmosis. You need a road map that shows you how to get from point A to point B.

Counseling and mentoring by others is certainly helpful, but in the final analysis you must draw your own map. Carefully survey the landscape before you and examine your options.

Be Flexible

A desired destination is absolutely meaningless without a clear map that shows you the best route. Then, once you are on the journey, anything can happen. Oh yes, a detour sign may appear, but it won't stop you if you know your target.

It's only after you have determined your goal that you devise a specific plan to see it develop into reality. Creating an "A,B,C" or "1,2,3" list may seem like a waste of time, but it is necessary as a clear step-by-step guide to your tomorrow.

Now comes the most important point. Your goal may seldom change, but your plan should always be flexible. This means that if Plan #1 doesn't work, there's no need to panic. In the process you have discovered essential information and now it's time to move to Plan #2. As the noted business writer Peter Drucker says, "Long range planning does not deal with future decisions, but with the future of present decisions.

Your goal may seldom change, but your plan should always be flexible.

"THIS IS THE DAY"

Please make certain your strategy includes a specific timetable for action. I've met people who repeatedly say they will reach their goal "someday":

- When the mortgage is paid off on the house.
- When they get the kids through college.
- When they have more time.

Don't procrastinate. Start now!

I encourage you to welcome each day with these words: *"This is the day which the Lord has made; I will rejoice and be glad in it"* (Psalm 18:24).

> *The greatest satisfaction is not necessarily in reaching your final goal, but in the joy of the journey.*

It is also vital to realize that the greatest satisfaction is not necessarily in reaching your final goal, but in the joy of the journey. So don't get upset if your target keeps moving like a mirage in the desert. Enjoy the achievement of every small mile marker on the exciting road you travel.

DOORS THAT OPEN—DOORS THAT CLOSE

Not every idea that pops into your head is right for you. But you will never know until you give it a try.

Before I was released from prison, I kept a notebook in my locker and would write down practically any thought or concept that came to mind.

As I read, I would take notes that inspired or

encouraged me, and write down quotations I wanted to remember. Some of these have made it into what you are now reading—but that was not my intent at the time.

One of my ideas was to start a gospel recording label upon my release. I had done some research and had numerous contacts in the industry from my time as an employee with a secular rap label during my college days. However, nothing I tried worked as I attempted to jump-start the record label. People were not receptive to my ideas, and some artists I planned to pursue had deals with other labels. As you can imagine, I became disheartened.

You see, God has specific plans for each of His children and He will close every door you try to open until you reach the one He has prepared just for you.

During this process, God continued to connect me with individuals who in the future would help me in my endeavors.

A Life-Changing Invitation

Believe you me, having a criminal record is rough

on a career. I lost not one but two well paying jobs because of what they discovered in the background check.

At one point I found myself married with a newborn baby, a mortgage and no income. I was deeply discouraged at the time.

Deavra, my entrepreneurial friend, asked me to pick up motivational speaker Les Brown from the airport for her. I was to take him and noted author and motivator Val Parker to a local radio station where they were to do an interview and promote a speaker series Deavra had organized through her nonprofit organization.

I realized that a golden opportunity had been dropped in my lap. The time I spent with Les, picking his brain about speaking to communicate effectively was invaluable.

As a result, he invited me to attend the Les Brown speakers training in Orlando, Florida.

However, because of my no-job status, I couldn't afford the registration fee—much less the hotel and flight to Florida.

Knowing such an opportunity may never come my way again, I borrowed a minimal amount of money from my family and made the trip.

THE DOLLAR MENU

The training was to take place at the beautiful Rosen Plaza Hotel, where most attendees were staying. Because of my lack of finances I had to find more modest accommodations at a motel about two miles away. It certainly wasn't the Rosen Plaza, but it served my purpose.

I spent a dollar each way on a tram going to and from the daily training sessions. When we broke for lunch (which I couldn't afford at the hotel), I walked about a quarter mile to McDonald's and ate off the dollar menu.

I felt the sacrifice was essential so I could receive the training I needed to take me to the next level of my development.

I felt the sacrifice was essential so I could receive the training I needed to take me to the next level of my development.

At night I would lie in bed in that motel room, thanking God for allowing me this opportunity to be a part of what we were experiencing at the conference. The sessions were very intense, and at times the speakers were overtaken by their own emotions. They believed passionately about inspiring and motivating people to live a purposeful, fulfilling life.

WRITE THE VISION

As a direct result of these sessions, I learned more about myself, what I wanted to accomplish, and what I was willing to do to achieve it.

One thing was clear to me. I needed to write my own story—the one you are holding in your hand. And I knew I should speak to men, women, and young people on how they can overcome their struggles.

My original goal was to help others, so I wasn't coming up with a new objective—only changing directions on how to reach the goal. So now I was putting the first three principles into action:

1. Stop Where You Are and Change Directions
2. Believe in Yourself and Your Abilities
3. Develop a Game Plan

Centuries ago, God told the prophet, Habakkuk, *"Write the vision and make it plain upon the tables, that he may run that read it"* (Habakkuk 2:2).

I obeyed this advice and put my vision into writing—a statement of where I was headed. Then I filled in the details—the plan—to make it happen.

I obeyed this advice and put my vision into writing.

Turning Goals into Action

Written words are powerful tools. They can bring you to tears, or bring you to a place of laughter. But hopefully, they will crystalize your purpose. In fact, the minute you "see" what you are seeking—even on a small piece of paper—it takes on a physical appearance.

In his book, *The Self-Talk Solution,* behavioral researcher, Shad Helmstetter, gives specific words we need to say regarding goal-setting and personal planning. They include "Anytime I want to make a change or achieve anything in my life, I write it down, along with my plan to accomplish the goal and when I will achieve it. In this way I turn each of my goals into action."

He also adds, "By writing out my goals, I am actually writing out my own script for the story of my future. By following my own specific action plan, I turn my dreams into reality."

These are words to live by.

PLAN TO WIN

What vision do you have hidden in your heart? It may be for you personally, for your family, for your finances, or for your spiritual life. Go ahead and start writing. Then post it in a prominent place where you can see it. Let it be a permanent, daily reminder of your goal.

This written statement will help keep you on track toward your desired objective.

Listen to what Les Brown calls "That still, quiet voice within." It will tell you what to include in your blueprint and which road to travel.

The saying holds true, "If you fail to plan, you plan to fail."

Proven Principle for Ultimate Success

#4

Discover Your Calling

Your calling will take you places you are celebrated not just tolerated.

– Bishop James Dixon II

One of the most rewarding things I have ever found in life is discovering that what I love to do is what God *wants* me to do.

My assignment on this earth is to uplift and encourage those who need it. I have been equipped with a personal story which serves as a warning to young people and offers hope and expectation to any person who has fallen into life's pit.

I once questioned God: "Why did I have to go to prison and suffer such terrible consequences?" He answered, *"Because you can handle it."*

WHY THE DEVIL ATTACKS

In my darkest days, Satan cast the spirit of fear upon me and those around me. But then, when I began to study scripture, I learned that God does not give us a spirit of fear (1 Timothy 1:7).

I remember the time in prayer when He said to me, "Fear not." Well, I was cool with that. In fact, I had known the Lord long enough to understand that if He had everything under control, it was taken care of and I didn't need to worry.

> *He probably wanted me to kill myself—or vent my wrath on someone else.*

I'm sure the devil was surprised and did not anticipate my calm reaction.

He probably wanted me to kill myself—or vent my wrath on someone else.

Let me make this clear. Every person Satan tries to

destroy is targeted for one simple reason. He or she has a divine calling to help encourage, and grow the Kingdom of God—period.

If you are not contributing anything to advance God's work on earth, you will most likely not be attacked. You are safe—off the hook, so to speak. On the other hand, if you are always catching hell for practically, everything you do, it's a good indication that you are on the verge of a spiritual breakthrough.

Once you discover your purpose and begin to pursue it, you will likely come under heavy enemy fire. So be warned!

An Unexpected Reward

I cannot count the number of times Satan has tried to make me doubt myself, my ability, and my calling. He has done it in many ways—using family, friends, my past, even my present circumstance to try and sabotage my divine assignment.

At one time, the devil had me fooled into thinking no school administrator would allow their students to be lectured to by an ex-offender. But I have spoken to hundreds of high school students on the importance of higher education and making better choices. Plus I get paid to do what I love!

When you realize your mission in life, you will be rewarded. I've received many invitations to speak to groups of all types. Initially I never set a fee for speaking, but I soon learned that most corporations, organization, and other groups have budgets set aside for individuals such as myself to make presentations. This became an unexpected source of income, a blessing from God. However, I would be thrilled and honored to share my story if I were not paid a dime.

Release the "Uncommon" You

In the biblical book of Ruth, the second chapter, there is a wonderful account of Boaz blessing Ruth because of her unselfishness.

Ruth and her mother-in-law, Naomi, had moved into a foreign land, but she volunteered to help in a harvest for which she was not being paid. Boaz, the prominent, wealthy landowner, saw Ruth as she diligently went out into the wheat fields, picking up the leftover grain behind the harvesters (Ruth 2:3).

Ruth did what was uncommon, and as a result, Boaz gave her special treatment—enough favor to meet the needs of both Ruth and her mother-in-law.

Please know that someone is always watching who can greatly bless you in your assignment.

A friend once told me, "Until you make an uncommon contribution into the earth, your existence is totally unnecessary."

Please know that someone is always watching who can greatly bless your assignment.

I try to live each day with this concept in mind. I may not always succeed, but I certainly try.

Allow me to encourage you to release what is "uncommon" from within you. How is this possible? First, realize the purpose for which you were placed on this planet. No one can reach their true potential plodding along doing the norm or what is considered "average." You will only be elevated to places of

Attached to every risk is a reward. celebration doing that which is extraordinary.

In the process, there is always a measure of risk. But the good news is that attached to every risk is a reward.

PURE INTENTIONS

I know a man who took every last dollar he had and added cash advances against his credit cards to start a trucking business. He even sold his car and his home because he believed in himself and his vision to such an extent that he knew his goal would be reached through hard work.

He asked for my thoughts concerning the huge step he was taking and his approach to achieving it. I simply asked him one question. "How will it advance God's Kingdom?"

He explained how he longed to sow more seed at his church to grow the ministry. His intentions were pure and God was faithful. Today, his church is thriving and so is his trucking business.

An Eternal Purpose

I have seen it all—the spectrum of many successes and failures. But I believe that in order for God to bless any project you undertake, there must be an eternal purpose at its core. In other words, there needs to be a heavenly reason for God to get involved in your mission.

> *If you make what is important to God important to you, God will make what is important to you important to Him.*

Here's how you should approach the issue: If you make what is important to God important to you, God will make what is important to you important to Him.

A Surprising Offer

I mentioned previously that someone is always watching your actions who can use their power, influence, and ability to help you in your assignment.

While working for a company in Houston, the Lord impressed upon my spirit that it was time to become involved in the real estate market.

My wife had recently passed the state real estate exam. I was so pumped up about a deal I was preparing to sign off on that I shared my excitement with one of my co-workers.

He was very quiet and listened intently as I went on and on about the details of the project. When I was finished, he pushed back in his chair and shared his own story with me of being in real estate almost twenty years earlier—how he made millions only to lose it all because of irresponsible behavior and sin.

> *"I've been watching you since you started working with the company."*

He told me that he had been selfish and had never shared his formula for success in real estate with any other person. He also let me know, "I've been watching you since you started with the company. I admire the way you carry yourself and go about your business."

I was surprised when the man told me that God

was directing him to go into business for himself again. Then he added, "Why don't you partner with me?"

He wanted to mentor and teach me everything he had learned about the industry. True to his word he did just that—and today I owe him a great deal of gratitude. He also taught me some of these faith principles I am sharing with you.

> *"When the student is ready, the teacher will appear."*

It reminds me of the saying, "When the student is ready, the teacher will appear."

Thank God, I was ready, willing, and able.

YOUR GIFTS OPEN DOORS

One of my favorite scriptures is Proverbs 18:16: *"A man's gifts will make room for him, and bring him before great men."*

Until I started writing this book, I had never connected that passage to what I had been already saying to myself in my daily faith confessions. I always ask God to bring me into the company of those who can use their power, influence, and ability to help me in a particular assignment.

The above scripture relates to what I say on a daily basis. I was unknowingly aligning myself with the Word of God, even before I knew what I was doing.

Once I responded to the Lord's urging to write this book, to encourage the downtrodden, and to motivate the hopeless, the Lord allowed me to see the manifestation of the words that I was speaking. Not only in my own life but also in the lives of those connected to me.

You will find this to be true for you. The Holy Spirit gives the words to say—and they will always line up with God's Word.

No Intimidation

When I discovered that part of my calling was to help others become financially independent through real estate, I had no idea how corrupt the industry is. But because the only real experience of negotiation I had under my belt was with drug dealers and arbitrating gang conflicts, I was not the least bit intimidated by bankers and loan brokers.

To this day, when in negotiations, I still take the approach that I am interviewing them to do business with my company, and not the other way around.

Imagine a banker's reaction when I walk in and announce, "We are interviewing banks today to determine who our company will do business with."

> *"We are interviewing banks today to determine who our company will do business with."*

In order for you to be effective with this technique you have to do your homework. Know your credit score; know your net worth; and know what the current interest rates are for the loan you are seeking.

Use Your Abilities

Without question, God wants to use our gifts for the benefit of His Kingdom and its agenda. Many people feel they have to "turn off" who they are to do heaven's work. But the Lord doesn't want mere robots. He made us all unique for a purpose.

Yes, your gift will make room for you.

Here is an example I like to use when speaking to ex-offenders:

> *"If you were incarcerated for drug trafficking or computer hacking, your management and programming skills and abilities are still needed in the Kingdom and should be used for Kingdom business. All churches need competent administrators, and information technology personnel. Use the talent God equipped you with to advance His work. As a result it will advance your calling."*

To most people, the word "hustler" is a derogatory term. I see it differently. In corporate America we call it networking. In hip hop culture the term is hustling. Therefore, in the Kingdom realm a hustler/networker should be connecting people who can help themselves and others in their ministry. So, if you were a hustler before you came to Christ, your hustle ability should now be used to benefit and advance the Kingdom of God.

What the devil means for evil, God can use for His glory.

Practically everything I had ever done which was negative, is now benefitting the One who originally purposed and planned my life—God Himself. Thankfully, I discovered my calling.

PROVEN PRINCIPLE FOR ULTIMATE SUCCESS

#5

FIND A SUCCESSFUL EXAMPLE TO FOLLOW

Keep away from people who try to belittle your ambitions. Small people always do that, the really great can make you feel that you, too, can become great.

– MARK TWAIN

I will be eternally grateful for those I have been able to call role models and mentors—my parents, my wife, my God-sister, my pastor, Les Brown, the list goes on. Each one of them has something unique they have deposited into me that makes me the man I am, and aspire to become.

Instructing—Coaching—Mentoring

In truth, there is a distinct difference between instructing, coaching, and mentoring:

- *Instructing* involves the dissemination of knowledge. It usually addresses the work at hand.
- *Coaching* primarily deals with skill building and career-related issues.
- *Mentoring* may include some of the above, but adds the element of helping to shape the attitude and outlook of the individual.

As you will discover, the mentoring relationship can be either formal or informal. A formal situation may include a group session, where several "mentees" are involved. When it's informal, there is usually just you and the mentor.

In the business world, we find formal mentoring for new employees, future leaders, and those believed to have high potential.

While this is highly desirable, nothing can replace a one-on-one relationship with a mentor who understands your vision and can use their experience and wisdom to help you reach yours.

Priceless Friendships

When I speak to groups of at-risk youth and talk about the issue of seeking out role models, the one question that continues to surface is, "How do you go about finding such a person?"

"How do you go about finding such a person?"

My answer is always the same. Look around you. They may be involved in the field of interest you desire to work in. They may be neighbors, friends, co-workers, or people you have yet to meet.

I remember talking to my wife, who had just become a licensed realtor, about another successful real estate agent she had read about in a local business publication. The woman had a stellar resume, so I urged Patricia to contact her and ask to be mentored. It sounded simple to me. After all, the agent could either say "yes" or "no."

As a result of one phone call, the woman invited my wife to lunch and to a speaking engagement at which she was to appear. The insights and information Patricia gained from this friendship was priceless.

"Take it By Force"

Prosperity is not accidental.

I cannot stress enough the importance of being fearless in your pursuit. Prosperity is not accidental. I will never forget a message Bishop Dixon preached entitled "A Violent Faith is a Victorious Faith." His theme was from a verse in the New Testament that reads: "And from the days of John the Baptist until now the kingdom of heaven suffereth violence, and the violent take it by force" (Matthew 11:12).

Success is not for the timid. You must be outspoken, even assert a certain swagger of assurance about yourself.

When I first started college I had a couple of strikes against me. As I look back, I had a chip on my shoulder and was arrogant. Plus, I struggled academically for the first time in my life.

To rectify the situation, I psyched myself out by singling out another classmate who excelled—and challenged myself to secretly do better than him on every assignment. I used him as my motivation and role model. I would say to myself, "If he can excel in this class, so can I."

A Silent Role Model

What motivates you toward achievement and success?

I recall a particular fraternity brother I went to college with. We came from the same background, same neighborhood, and same high school. I looked to him for motivation because he was a year ahead of me. I constantly thought, "If he can make it, then surely I can too."

He was an up-close example of who I wanted to

become. I don't believe he even knew how tremendously helpful he was to me during that time. Even though I have not been in contact with him since college days, I pray that he will one day read these words and know the impact he had on me.

In this case, the role model did not know he had been selected for such an assignment.

"SERIAL" DREAM KILLERS

Before you share your vision, choose a person of good character who has been successful in the arena in which you desire to operate.

Pessimistic people are dream destroyers.

Once you discover your calling do everything in your power to stay away from negative influences.

Pessimistic people are dream destroyers. They most likely have not fulfilled their purpose because of lack of effort and are now "serial killers" of anyone's dream they come in contact with.

When you meet such an individual, always speak

positively, but guard your ideas from them. Why? Whatever plans you share for your future, they will discourage you from doing—giving every possible reason why your idea will fail and not succeed.

You may not be able to name anyone in your circle of friends and peers who is a dream killer, possibly because you have not shared your vision with them. But the moment you do, they will identify themselves by their negative words.

Treat them with love and prayer. Remember, we are to *"follow those who through faith and patience inherit the Kingdom of God"* (Hebrew 6:12).

PROVEN PRINCIPLE FOR ULTIMATE SUCCESS

#6

HAVE A RIGHTEOUS RESOLVE

When faced with a mountain, I will not quit! I will keep striving until I climb over, find a pass through, tunnel underneath—or simply stay and turn the mountain into a gold mine, with God's help.
— ROBERT H. SCHULLER

In order for God to bless us with wealth and prosperity we must first—before even praying and asking for it—have a Righteous Resolve. What do I mean by this statement? We must have a settled purpose that is pleasing to God so He can honor our request.

I cannot count the number of times I have been moved to sow a financial "faith seed" for a ministry project at our church. As you may have already concluded, the word "faith" before "seed" means I was making a commitment to give something I didn't already possess—an amount of money I had to believe the Lord for.

Time after time, I have been able to give to God's work because He blessed me in unexpected ways.

God's Obligation

He is obligated to make sure what you ask for comes to pass.

It is my experience that the Lord will never allow you or your household to go lacking when you have this kind of Righteous Resolve. First, He is obligated to make sure what you ask for comes to pass. Second, He already wants to see you blessed. But above all, the Kingdom must be financed and the resources flow through His children. Yet, He is active on our behalf, As scripture states, "*But thou shall remember the Lord thy God: for it is he that giveth the power to get wealth*" (Deuteronomy 8:18).

God responds to our faith demands. We must, however, have a reason that is on the Kingdom agenda. The Lord desires to exceed our expectations so very much that He anxiously waits for our request. He longs to bless us abundantly, so others will look at our success and be amazed!

When I share my story, I often hear the response, "That had to be God."

An Amazing Sequence

None of what we have discussed so far will take place if we do not practice the principle of having a Righteous Resolve.

Financially, my prayer has been, "Lord, give me more so I can give You more."

Please believe me when I tell you that God will

only get finances and blessing *to* you, if He can get them *through* you. If the Lord can trust you to give back to Him what He gave you (through tithes and offerings), then He will pour out additional abundance.

WHERE IT BEGINS

> *Our heavenly Father is never motivated to move because of our own selfish desires.*

Our heavenly Father is never motivated to move because of our own selfish desires. Everything we do must be to glorify Him and to advance the Kingdom and His ministry. Once these requirements are met, then we will be blessed from the overflow. The words Jesus said long ago are still true: *"Give, and it will be given to you: good measure, pressed down, shaken together, and running over will be put into your bosom. For with the same measure that you use, it will be measured back to you"* (Luke 6:38).

What an exciting promise! Think about having sufficient resources that you can give to God abundantly and still have more than enough to meet your needs. It all begins with your Righteous Resolve to give.

God Knows Your Heart

I have proven this myself, but let me tell you how a businessman friend of mine saw this materialize in his own life.

He wanted to sow a seed of $5,000 into his church on what they called Impact Sunday. However, when the time came, it became obvious to him that he was going to be about $1,200 short of his pledge commitment because his mortgage was due.

He told me how he had prayed about it and the Lord knew he wanted to fulfill his obligation to both his lender and to the ministry.

Then, on Friday before Impact Sunday, he received a phone call from the company that financed his home, saying, "Because of your track record, we would like to offer you and several other homeowners the opportunity to skip this month's payment and tack it to the end of the loan. Would you like to take advantage of this?"

You know the answer. As a result, he was able to honor his faith pledge.

God knew his heart and that his desire was genuine—thereby clearing the path for him to bless the church.

Motivated to Move

The key to success and abundance lies in all of the principles we have talked about. One doesn't work without the others, but having a Righteous Resolve is essential—and I hold it in high esteem.

I am convinced that if this principle is not mastered, the others are rendered ineffective. When the Lord knows your intentions are sincere, He will "make a way where there is no way." His ability to act on your behalf will be unobstructed.

Let me stress the fact that God has to be motivated to move. If we never ask the Lord to get involved in our lives, He won't. Instead, He will simply sit on the sidelines until we invite Him to come in. He is not an intrusive God, rather, His desire is to bless us above and beyond what we can think or imagine (Ephesians 3:20).

> *If we never ask the Lord to get involved in our lives, He won't.*

So often we prevent our heavenly Father from helping and blessing us because we have not met the criteria for Him to do so. Most of us never welcome Him into our situations. Though it hurts Him to sit and watch us not live up to our potential, He will not get involved until we invite Him. We do this by acknowledging we can't accomplish anything by ourselves—that He is "God Almighty."

A Divine Determination

When it comes to righteousness or being resolute, you may wonder, "Which comes first?"

I believe that our resolve is a direct result of righteous living. Long ago, King Solomon wrote, *"The righteous will never be uprooted, but the wicked will not remain in the land"* (Proverbs 10:30).

When your roots are firmly established in faith, absolutely nothing can pull you away. You know beyond any shadow of doubt that you have been appointed and anointed for the mission you have been given.

> *When your roots are firmly established in faith, absolutely nothing can pull you away.*

God will give you a divine determination not only to run the race, but to win. I love the words of the apostle Paul: *"Do you not know that those who run in a race all run, but one receives the prize? Run in such a way that you may obtain it"* (1 Corinthians 9:24).

It Starts with You!

If you are waiting for the Lord to initiate the first

step, you will be waiting for a lifetime. It all starts with you!

You don't receive until you ask. For example, at a place called Gibeon, God asked Solomon, in a dream at night, *"Ask! What shall I give you?"* (1 Kings 3:5). Jesus said, *"Ask, and it will be given to you; seek, and you will find; knock, and it will be opened to you"* (Matthew 7:7).

Regardless of what we desire from heaven, we have to make the first move: *"Come to Me, all you who labor and are heavy laden, and I will give you rest"* (Matthew 11:28).

Even the amazing gift of salvation itself requires action (belief) on our part: *"For God so loved the world that He gave His only begotten Son, that whoever believes in Him should not perish but have everlasting life"* (John 3:16).

DON'T FORGET THE "IF"

We all want blessings to rain down from heaven, but God's gifts are conditional. I smile when I hear people talk of all the promises they read about in scripture—how they will receive abundance, protection, favor, and the list goes on. But they fail to realize there is an "if" involved. In fact, the word "if" is used over 1,500 times in the Bible. It is only "if" we obey God's commands that His promises are ours.

> *The word "if" is used over 1,500 times in the Bible.*

- *"If you will indeed obey My voice and keep My covenant, then you shall be a special treasure to Me above all people"* (Exodus 19:5).

- *"If you earnestly obey My commandments which I command you today, to love the Lord your God and serve Him with all your heart and with all your soul, then I will give you the rain for your land in its season"* (Deuteronomy 11:13-14).

- *"If you are willing and obedient, you shall eat the good of the land"* (Isaiah 1:19).

- *"If you have faith as a mustard seed, you will say to this mountain, 'Move from here to there,' and it will move; and nothing will be impossible for you"* (Matthew 17:20).

- *"If you abide in My word, you are My disciples indeed"* (John 8:31).

- *"If anyone keeps My word he shall never see death"* (John 8:51).

- *"Therefore, if anyone is in Christ, he is a new creation; old things have passed away; behold, all things have become new"* (2 Corinthians 5:17).

Have you met the conditions?

Favor from Above

What gives you the strength, courage, and faith to take the "IF" step? It comes by (1) acknowledging we can do nothing by ourselves, (2) that He is God Almighty, and (3) that we have the Righteous Resolve He requires to release His blessings.

Remember, you are a child of the King and have favor with your heavenly Father.

Proven Principle for Ultimate Success

#7

Possess the Palace

For he has come out of prison to become king, even though he was born poor in his kingdom.

– Ecclesiastes 4:14

For centuries, writers have chronicled the stories of men and women who have gone from rags to riches, from poverty to prosperity, from tragedy to triumph.

My journey from a prison cell to a place of purpose is not new. In fact, one of the most powerful stories ever recorded is the true account of a dreamer who was literally thrown into an earthly pit, before making one of the most dramatic comebacks in history.

The Dreamer

Let me introduce you to a young man named Joseph. He was the eleventh of twelve sons, and his father, Jacob, loved him more than the rest. He even had a special, colorful coat made for him. You can read all about it in Genesis 37-50.

As you can imagine, the favoritism shown by their father made Joseph's brothers extremely jealous.

One night, Joseph dreamed that he and his brothers were out in the field binding corn—and his brother's bundles were bowing down to his bundle. Another night he dreamed that the sun, moon, and stars bowed down to him.

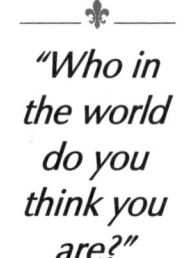

Well, when Joseph shared his dreams with his brothers, you can imagine the jealousy of his siblings. "Who in the world do you think you are?" they questioned.

> *"Who in the world do you think you are?"*

Immediately, the brothers began to plot for a way to get rid of Joseph.

Shortly after, when they were all away from their

home, the angry brothers threw Joseph into an empty well. But just before tossing him into this pit, they tore off his coat of many colors which Jacob had given him.

TWENTY PIECES OF SILVER

Then, while they were sitting nearby, eating a meal, a caravan of merchants passed by headed for Egypt. Their camels were loaded with spices and perfumes.

The brothers said, "What good will come from killing Joseph and trying to conceal the evidence. Let's sell him to these Ishmaelites." They sold him for twenty pieces of silver and the merchants took Joseph with them to Egypt.

The brothers returned home, but before they did, they killed a goat and dipped his coat in the blood. When they showed the garment to Jacob, he cried,"My son's coat!—A wild animal has eaten Joseph."

Jacob cried and mourned for many days.

Thrown into Prison

On arrival in Egypt, the merchants sold Joseph as a slave to a man named Potiphar, one of Pharaoh's officials, manager of his household affairs.

He didn't remain a slave long. In fact, Potiphar was so impressed with this young man he placed him in charge of everything he owned.

Joseph was a handsome man and one day Potiphar's wife made a play for him. Joseph refused her many advances, but one day, furious at his rejection, she grabbed his robe, ran out of the house and lied that Joseph had tried to seduce her.

Immediately, Joseph was thrown in prison.

What Could this Mean?

After being behind bars a lengthy time, two fellow prisoners, a baker and a cupbearer to Pharaoh each had a dream. They came to Joseph to learn the interpretation—and he told the cupbearer that he would soon be freed. Joseph also said, "When you are released, please tell Pharoah about me."

Well, after walking out of prison, the cupbearer quickly forgot all about Joseph. But two years later, Pharaoh had two dreams that no one could explain.

In his first dream he saw seven healthy cows and seven scrawny cows coming out of the Nile river. The second dream concerned seven ears of grain growing out of a single stalk. Then seven more ears grew up, but they were thin and dried. Amazingly, the thin ears swallowed up the healthy ears.

When Pharaoh awoke, he called for all the sages and magicians of Egypt, but no one could explain what this meant.

Fortunately, the cupbearer remembered what Joseph had done for him and Joseph was brought to the palace. They gave him a haircut and new clothes so he was presentable.

"I understand you can interpret dreams."

Pharaoh said, "I understand you can interpret dreams."

Joseph replied, "I can't, but God can."

The Coming Famine

Immediately, Joseph told Pharaoh that both dreams meant the same thing. The seven healthy cows and ears of grain meant seven years of plenty. And the seven sick cows and scrawny ears of grain meant seven years of famine.

He informed Pharaoh he had only seven years to stockpile for the coming devastation.

Joseph then said, "You need to look for a wise and experienced man and put him in charge of the country during these years of plenty."

Pharaoh, looked at his officers and announced, "I believe this is the man we need. Where else can we find a person with God's Spirit in him?"

"Where else can we find a person with God's Spirit in him?"

On the spot, Joseph was commissioned by Pharaoh—who went so far as to remove his signet ring and put in on Joseph's hand. He was given the finest robes and a gold chain was placed around his neck.

At the age of thirty, Joseph was now living in a

palace and running the government of Egypt; second only to Pharaoh.

For the next seven years, Joseph prepared Egypt for the upcoming famine. When it arrived, he began opening up the storehouses—and people journeyed from many neighboring nations because the famine was so widespread.

The Brothers Bowed

Back in Canaan, Jacob and his family were hungry, so he told his sons to travel to Egypt to buy food. Of course, they had to come directly before Joseph, who was running the country. As they bowed at his feet—just as Joseph had seen in his first dream—he immediately recognized them, but spoke roughly and treated them as strangers, even accusing them of being spies.

The brothers, not knowing who they bowed before, returned home with food, but the famine became so bad they had to return to Egypt for a second visit.

On this encounter, Joseph was deeply moved and had to go into another room and cry.

The time finally came when Joseph could not hold back his identity any longer. He revealed himself with the words, "I am Joseph, your brother whom you sold into slavery. Is my father still alive?"

As they drew closer, Joseph told them not to feel guilty or blame themselves for what they did. "You see, God sent me here to save lives—to make sure there was a remnant in the land."

They ran back to Jacob with the amazing news, and the entire family, along with their flocks, were soon reunited in Egypt.

The brothers, still filled with remorse, begged, "Please let us be your slaves." But Joseph replied, *"You meant evil against me, but God meant it for good, in order to bring it about as it is this day, to save many people alive"* (Genesis 50:20).

Joseph knew the hand of the Lord was with

him—from the pit to the palace—and he treated his brothers with love and respect.

Your Place of Purpose

I believe the day is on the horizon when you will move into the place God has prepared just for you.

Please let me give you this advice. When you take possession of the palace, you have to own it. You must be confident in the fact that you belong there.

> *When you take possession of the palace, you have to own it.*

Sadly, many have been confined in their pits so long they have convinced themselves that great success is not God's plan for their lives.

We must realize that we were created to live in the palace. At first it may not seem to fit you well because you are unfamiliar with all its unique features, but once you have been there awhile you will begin to realize that this mansion was built with you in mind.

This is *your* place of purpose—not meant for anyone else.

> *Your orientation does not determine your destination.*

Millions have been conditioned to think they are not worthy of living in such surroundings. But your orientation does not determine your destination. Get this truth down deep in your spirit so it will carry you forward until your faith catches up with your future.

You Deserve It!

In his inspiring book, *Live Your Dream,* Les Brown says, "Go after your dream with a sense of entitlement. Know that you have the power to achieve it and that you deserve it. Be willing to get up into life's face, grab it by the collar and say, 'Give it UP! It's my dream.'"

According to Les, "Whatever you accomplish in life is not a manifestation so much of what you *do*, as what you believe deeply within yourself that you *deserve*." And he adds, "You have to focus on yourself and sell yourself on the ability to perform, to achieve your objectives and to *deserve* them. Tell yourself when you review your goals each day that you deserve them. Say to yourself, *'I'm capable, talented; I'm committed. I DESERVE my goals.'*

Say farewell to the pit. Say hello to the palace!

A Final Word

I believe that somewhere on these pages you have seen a picture of yourself. Perhaps you can recall a time when you were trapped so deep in one of life's pits that you never believed you could escape. Or it may be that you have climbed to the surface and are looking for a way to fulfill your dreams.

Let me encourage you to read this book again and again until the Seven Principles for Ultimate Success are so deeply etched into your thinking that their practice becomes a daily habit.

- If you are stuck in a rut, have you made the decision to change directions?
- Do you truly believe in yourself and your abilities?
- Have you developed a personal game plan for success?
- Have you discovered your true calling and purpose in life?

- Have you identified a role model to follow or chosen a mentor?
- Do you have a righteous resolve to do things God's way?
- Have you claimed the palace you deserve?

It is my prayer these words have inspired you to see your dream fulfilled—not years from now, but soon. Thankfully, we have the assurance that it's God's desire for us to live in abundance on this earth and for eternity.

Jesus tells us, *"In My Father's house are many mansions; if it were not so, I would have told you. I go to prepare a place for you. And if I go and prepare a place for you, I will come again and receive you to Myself; that where I am, there you may be also"* (John 14:2-3).

Your palace doors are waiting to swing open wide.

NOTES

For Additional Resources
or to Schedule the Author for
Speaking Engagements, Contact:

Darrell Barnes

Phone: 832-347-6525
Email: pit.palace@gmail.com
Internet: www.darrellbarnes.com

Please contact the author to purchase or sponsor quantities of this book to be given to at-risk young people or those in prison.